P9-CSE-326

LIGHT

S Thammavongsa

LIGHT | SOUVANKHAM THAMMAVONGSA

PEDLAR PRESS | St John's

COPYRIGHT © 2013
Souvankham Thammavongsa

ALL RIGHTS RESERVED. No part
of this book may be reproduced or
transmitted in any form or by any
means whatsoever without written
permission from the publisher, except
by a reviewer, who may quote brief
passages in a review. For information,
write Pedlar Press at 113 Bond Street,
St John's NL A1C 1T6 Canada.

ACKNOWLEDGEMENTS
The publisher wishes to thank the
Canada Council for the Arts and the
Ontario Arts Council for their generous
support of our publishing program.

LIBRARY AND ARCHIVES CANADA
CATALOGUING IN PUBLICATION

Thammavongsa, Souvankham, 1978-,
author
    Light / Souvankham Thammavongsa.

Poems.
ISBN 978-1-897141-56-4 (pbk.)

I. Title.

PS8589.H3457L54   C811'.6
C2013-903178-2

COVER ART Catharine Nicholson,
The Viable (2008), pen and ink on
watercolour paper

BOOK DESIGN
Zab Design & Typography

TYPEFACE
Garamond

Printed in Canada

ACKNOWLEDGEMENTS

Thank you to the Corporation of
Yaddo for a residency during which
some of these poems were written.

To the Canada Council for the Arts,
Toronto Arts Council, Ontario
Arts Council Writers' Reserve and
Works in Progress programs for
encouragement and support.

To the editors of the following
publications in whose pages these
poems first appeared: *Canadian
Literature*: "Fie"; *Contemporary
Verse 2*: "Agnes Martin, Untitled
#10"; *dANDelion*: "The Turtle";
Echolocation: "The Dung
Beetle"; *Event*: "Perfect"; *The
Fiddlehead*: "Dream"; *The Puritan*:
"I Remember"; *Rusty Toque*:
"Lightning Storm Seen From the
Window of An Airplane"; *The
Week Shall Inherit The Verse*: "At the
Farm"; *The Windsor Review Best
Under 35 Issue*: "A Sparkle-Scale
Sunrise," "Colossal Squid," and
"The Fish in Mammoth Cave."

"The Turtle" and "The Ostrich"
were published in a limited edition
chapbook by greenboathouse books
in 2006. Thanks to Jason Dewinetz
and Aaron Peck. "The Scarecrow"
was published in a limited edition
chapbook by Junction Books in
2001. Many thanks to Carleton
Wilson. "The Sun in Flannery
O'Connor's *The Violent Bear It Away*"
and "A Straight Line" (as "This Is the
Direction") appeared in the anthology
*Troubling Borders: Southeast Asian
Women in the Diaspora* published by
the University of Washington Press.
Thank you to Lan Duong.

Thank you to my family and to my
good friends. To Heather Hugginson
for all these years. To Malcolm
Woodland for the usual reasons. To
Paramita Nath, for a long time. To
Christopher Nicholson and Zab
Hobart. To Beth Follett, specially. To
Dionne Brand, always. And to my
husband, Andrew DuBois, for the
rest of it.

CONTENTS

LIGHT

This is a clearing: a rule
you will bind to yourself like a promise
to begin

It's the colour bone is when you take it
out of itself, the colour of cold
when the sun doesn't come to its calling

It's the shape and shapes water
could be, the direction light can travel
to get to you

It's the plot and path
of a small single letter,
the face of a country you can make yours:

the lines, the grids, the marks are here

LJÓS

In Icelandic the word for light is ljós

And the word for poem is ljóð

What happens at the end can change everything

One ending starts in the middle, makes a left, circles back slightly off mark, then makes a right, slides a little further down and ends in the middle again, looking back at where it's been, knowing exactly how far it has come

The other ending starts in the middle too, drops down, finds its way back and then goes further, pointing a sword at some high heaven, never looking back

It is said everything in the universe contains the same matter

That we begin somewhere in the same place

The matter responsible is as close as one last end veering off

This is how you say fire in Lao

Anything that has light must acknowledge *that first fire*

Fie mie is fire when it's burning something down

A house burns down, a forest, a city

Fie sang is flashlight

A man-made object, a thing you take out into that not-knowing

Fie fa is thunder

That scrawl of light in the shape broken things first take

Fie mot is what happens when you're not expecting it

A power outage, a burnt bulb

Mot fie is when you do something to light

It's a far reach, set above you, a calling out of place

It's a turn, a switch in the wall you go to find

Fie mot

Mot fie

It will be different here. You can take a leap
off this ledge ten feet and never touch
ground. You can hover in what

could be air, lean back further and further
and something that feels like faith
will lift, will hold you up. But it isn't faith,

it's some kind of physics, law, a rule of matter
put in place, set in place
as old and as constant as that sun:

that unsettled speck, that shadowless thing,
that thing to have.

Last winter fishermen caught a giant squid
off the coast of New Zealand and sold it to

a museum for scientific study and research.
It was said that if you cut it up and fried it

it would taste like ammonia. It was said it is
rather rare to find a squid this size. They were

hoping this one was female because the one
they had in the lab was male. They said the

eyes were the size of "dinner plates" and
could absorb a great amount of light. Why

this was important had something to do with
where it lived, where there was no light at all.

SWAN

Half its body has been sunk
and its head drooped so

low it looks to be the beginning of
a question mark

At this distance, its legs take
the shape of an unmoving dot

though up close it is working up
a scribble of tiny uneven circles

Up close, clumps, wet feathers,
line upon line

of long white eyelashes flap loose in
the cold of a winter sun

Up close, a cracked beak
and one eye set far back

A sparkle
so tiny

and in its brilliance
so brave

took
what there was

left
of light

and threw it
high

never
minding

there wasn't
a sky

that could hold it
there

Here, it bursts
  into blood
and fire
  or rises

calm
  and contained;
slips
  over thin lines

of trees;
  or circles
and circles
  in a yellow haze

And here, it is
  a blister,
furious
  and hot,

too
  far away
to ignite
  anything

PERFECT

When I am fourteen, my father will quit
his job and sell our home. He will use the money
to start a sign-making business. He will start
by buying computers and big heavy equipment
and we will spend nights sleeping in the van.
I'll try my best to sleep, to close my eyes
and feel warm in my wet socks and thin winter coat.
In the mornings, I'll brush my teeth at school
and comb my hair so I'll look like nothing is wrong
with me. I'll wander the empty dark halls
before the students fill them, and sometimes
I'll sing and dance like a star in a Broadway play.
When I see a teacher, I'll sit quietly outside
a classroom door with a heavy book in my hand.
Moby-Dick. The only teacher to ask
is Ms. Irons. I will tell her that I'm just
so excited for school and I'm so happy to be here.
It's not a lie. I'm happy that for the whole
of a day, I'll be warm and I can be with my friends.
I don't tell her all the other stuff. That this will be
the year my parents' marriage will begin to fall apart.
That they'll stop dancing in the living room
and that my mother will stop making me beautiful dresses
which match hers from leftover materials,
that the bottles full of colour and fragrances dry up.
I didn't know it then so how could I tell her?
After school, my mother will pick me up and drive
for hours. She'll sometimes stop at a lake somewhere
in cottage country and listen to the radio. She'll walk
back and forth, never saying anything. And I
will bow my head and work out the math problems
in my homework. The math problems are easy.

They are always about some guy who had to get
to the other side. There's always an answer, a sure thing.
You just have to work your way there. Everything
you need to know to solve it has already been given
to you. There is no secret but the answer,
shimmering alone without any signs around it.
I will keep my print small, filling up every blank space
I can find like a Captain plugging leaks in a sinking ship.
It will get dark and just as the sun sets,
the streetlamp will turn on. I will angle
my notebook to catch this light. This light.
I will go back to school and hand in my notebook
and it will be perfect. Perfect. It's what I've earned.
A friend will lean in and announce my score,
and I'll hear someone ask, "How'd *you* get perfect?"
I can't begin to say what it took to get it that way.
It's perfect. Perfect.

THE DARK

is light

when light

isn't here

It comes

in

the same way:

takes up

what light left,

and makes

sure

to this

it comes back

Toss your bright paper-punched confetti
into air

Jump up and down and skip around by
the shore

Pose and spread yourself and extend and then give
all away

Confess about the little pretty dotted details of your life
scratch them

and string them along a cliff wall so they will last for ever and
ever and ever

Then pack your lungs thick and wide and deep
with all this

and go out there, *there*, where you think
you belong

open wide into that light
and tell us again what you think you've got

It means you are light, that you can begin differently now, that you've taken it all off

It means to show your tooth and claw, without the work, the polish, the appointment

If the ending were different, if you placed the last letter right after the beginning, it would be an animal, a power, a warning from which to stay away

Face to face, maybe you'd see they're really not all that different, both just trying

A rearrangement, a shift, a move out of place, a spine realigned

But it would take that wouldn't it? That face to face, to know

A STAR

is a sugar-grained

sprinkle

of light

thrown

to dot

a darkened sky

takes

the sun in

and in

it rises

to take

itself

up

It says this light bulb will last one year

Its light output is 830 lumens, its life is 1,500 hours, it uses 60 watts

A Buddhist Temple is called a wat

It never gets replaced and one is never built to look just like the other

Every candle inside is a lit prayer and glows at the centre ever more bright

Its light output in lumens and its life hours haven't been marked down

To keep it going, someone somewhere is keeping a count, preparing a return

THE TURTLE

sawn

in half,

was left only

its upper shell;

crutched

underneath this,

its spine;

and below this,

where reason

might have stood, a clearing

THE OSTRICH

born

winged

and beaked,

bones set

for flight

and dash,

watches

like the rest of us

A FEATHER IS LIGHT

At the centre of it
here is bone

you can see through,
thin

as a plastic straw,
narrowing

to close itself up
at the ends

And all along
this bone,

smaller black feathers
line themselves,

their bones,
sharpened and thinned,

mend like needles

THE DUNG BEETLE

has been given

this

all its life

and all its life

it has quietly sifted and culled

each bit, each piece

As if

each bit, each piece

had been lost to us,

a lesser light

dropped

from pinned points

in the night sky

Each bit, each piece

rounded up

and rounded out

a circle

to be made solid

A circle

it will one day be called upon

to drag up

into the open

and set

for the rest of us

a rising sun

The Arabic word for light

Two circles sit side by side

Twins, equal in size and shape and the space they both contain

They had been made to be like each other

Up there, one contains all light

Kept at a distance, as far away as a lost love, a hope long past, an apology that changes nothing

The other by its proximity seems only to have light, a compass for the sun, a backseat to, a smaller sidekick

On this sheet of paper, these two circles look to be the same, as close in likeness as they could ever be

Stripped of light, one is like the other, as small, as equal, as alone

THE SUN DOES NOT KNOW

what

    it is like

        to be cold,

    or how

      to take in

that dark

    around it

And it doesn't even know

what it looks like

to each of us

in our turn,

at its rise,

at its set

DREAM

We were all dressed up and on our way
to something like a wedding. I saw two cars
following each other down an unpaved road.
By this unpaved road, I saw my father lying
on a green-grass hill, dressed in a dark wool suit.
He looked like he was twenty-five years old.
His black hair had grown full around his head
and he was thin like the young usually are.
He was just lying there and I didn't know why
he was like that but began to understand a bit
when I saw a groundskeeper cover him
with clear plastic like the kind that comes with
new furniture. I got out of the car and went to
my father and picked up his light-boned body
and held him like he was my child. Suddenly
his body slipped down the hill. His arms went first
like he was doing a backward dive into a pool
and I quickly grabbed his arms and arranged them
at his side. Now I knew he was dead and tried
to fix his arms to his side so he would look respectable
here without a coffin. My mother and my brother
were there too, but useless, crying and too young
to understand. My mother wore a white silk dress,
made-up, and my brother was still four years old here,
though he had just celebrated his thirtieth year.
They are watching me now and want me to say
something, explain what's happened to us,
give some final speech. But I say nothing.

The houses rise up overnight,
brushing over fields of dandelions,
bright circles
soon to be grey fluff.
It seems the swans
don't know it yet.
The reservoir now a parking lot,
row upon row of outlines of white.
Ever loyal to daylight and rain
but never quite knowing how hard the storm,
soaked and stooped,
they keep their manners
in all of this. They still come out, preened,
their long white necks bending,
a curtain call, a curtsy,
bending and bowing down,
bowing down, down low for bits of that sun.

A cluster fell to the ground in a small heap, tossed out like bits of unused black fabric

They fell slow and in small batches like ash tapped from the end of a burning cigarette

Any sudden move made a handful leap back, back into that blue upturned tray, that dump, that ash-receiver

Everything you see now will survive the winter and its cold

Ash is what a fire leaves behind when it's done

This fire isn't done, forming and tumbling through some dark

The ash that is here, a small cluster of red spheres bundled together

Whatever we know of fire, we know it is not done

Or could it be that it *is* done? That ash can have colour like life?

That ash isn't the final stage but the performance of a beginning

LIGHTNING STORM SEEN FROM THE WINDOW OF AN AIRPLANE

Where once there swirled cottons of soft white and various hues of blue

Some bent metal wire charged and flickered inside an incandescent bulb

Some fly fisher's line pulled at by one who didn't know how to fly cast

Some flame-thrower's flame tossed over and over and over by itself

Some length of shining white ribbon wrapped around a ball come loose

Some strands of copper-coloured tinsel dangled from what wasn't there

POSTCARD

The real hour of the day is not known

The sky is blue-grey

The snow is flat in these fields

Bare trees line themselves along the horizon like shards from black glass

The sun, if it will rise today, will begin on the left

Every shape of cloud has been here once

In an hour, the buildings will be the first to rise into view

Each building, a neat ordering of glass and light

Nearby a needle sticks out

Two circles at the pointed end, a thread-through, the start of a beading

These circles are different in size

They do nothing but offer us a different view of ourselves

An assemblage of pretty dots and moving bits

Into this, we are coming for the real hour of the day

I was sitting in the car counting the black flies

They had come in through the open window

There were four

One was on the rear-view mirror

The other three were perched on my left hand

I heard a gunshot by the barn and thought nothing of it

We were at a farm

I saw a cow come charging forward with its head half gone

A man with an axe came running behind it

He hit it once

Once he hit it

And it fell to the ground

Everything was eaten

Its eye appeared in a soup that night

Everything accounted for

PARSLEY

All lean
in the same
direction
as if
some event
outside
needed witness,
as if
bleacher-full
all were there
to cheer on
some long-awaited
victory,
some goal,
some hometown-hero
touchdown

I remember Hopscotch and roller skates.

I remember when my father learned to roller skate. He fell on his right cheek and it turned plum-purple.

I remember my parents practicing ballroom dancing in the living room. My mother wore a twirly skirt and my father wore his black *souliers*. The carpet they danced on was green like grass.

I remember my brother laughing so hard, a giant green booger landed in the sand in the playground.

I remember asking for a picture of a boy I liked. He signed the back of it like he was famous. I just wanted the picture.

I remember going to Sunday School and being asked to leave. I was colouring paper-cut angels which formed a king's crown. I was wearing it when I left the class.

I remember learning to ride a two-wheeler without the training wheels. It was pink and had a basket in front, but I never put anything in there.

I remember burying pennies in the ground, thinking they'd grow into trees just because I was told they didn't. I wanted to see for myself.

I remember someone at school told me a bee could still sting you even though it was dead. I saw a dead one behind the curtain and touched the stinger. It's true. It can sting you.

I remember being on a swing and swinging toward a bumblebee. It could not be avoided. It hit the centre of my forehead and fell to the ground, bouncing like a rubber ball. I got off the swing to take a look at it. It lay in the sand, still. I was embarrassed for the thing. It didn't have a chance.

I remember dissecting a white rat. I pinned it down and broke two of its joints. The instructions said to start the cut at the hole near its back. My lab partner, Brian, turned his head away and said he didn't want to do it. I wanted to impress him and picked up the scissors and shoved them in. Cut open, there was a brown sack, the shape of an earlobe. I took it out, labelled it, and cut that open too. It gave off a bad smell. I knew then, it had to be the stomach. A heart couldn't hold that kind of rot.

I remember fitting my size five feet into size three shoes just because they were cheaper.

I remember riding the bus for fifty cents.

I remember yo-yos and hula hoops.

I remember when my co-worker got married. He left his computer password on a yellow notepad for me and said he'd be back in a week.

I remember throwing out my red running shoes and Vincent, who lived next to the laundry room of the apartment building, returning them to me because he knew they were mine. He tied the laces.

I remember a friend stealing a dictionary from the classroom for me because she knew I didn't have one at home and that I wanted one. She took it out of her knapsack and gave it to me in the parking lot. We climbed a metal fence and on the other side we started to run like we were being chased, but no one was after us.

I remember auditioning for Little Red Riding Hood in a school play. It was the scene after the wolf told me he would eat me. I fell to the ground and pretended to die. I stuck my tongue out at the corner of my mouth to look dead, but I didn't get the part.

I remember telling my Home Ec teacher I wanted to be a model. She said I was too short. She hung her lingerie in the classroom and flirted with the repairman. She taught us how to cook pizza and pigs-in-a-blanket. We baked cakes and they always collapsed in the middle.

I remember handwriting.

I remember buying a lot of white dresses. When I got married I wore none of those.

I remember when I had to dial a phone.

I remember when I had a pen pal in Loon Rapids, Minnesota. We wrote three letters to each other and then I sent him a photograph of me. He never wrote back after that.

A young man
in the courtyard is singing

I don't know what
he looks like
but he has a good voice, a young voice

He's singing Michael Jackson's
Man in the Mirror

Just the chorus

It makes me think of
a Michael Jackson button I had in Grade Two

I hid it in my coat pocket
and took it out to kiss it whenever
no one was looking

After some time
his face began to disappear

My mother always said
never to love a thing too much

A STRAIGHT LINE

It's hard to tell
   at this point
where it's going
   and where it's been

The bit you see
   could be the beginning
of something
   or the end of another

It's too soon
   or too late to tell
what it was
   before it got here

It could be
   counting on you
or counting you in
   or something already gone

Whatever you think it is
   remember what it looks like
because a word
   begins this way

Still light.
Next door, there is a small cat,
long white hair
with patches of black.

It knows
to go out there,
the few hours when
the trains don't run.
Along a single rail
it balances its weight
careful, controlled, a tightrope walker.

At night, it walks the whole block
quiet and deliberate.
You can tell
if it loves you by what it brings
to the front door. The part
of the mouse it leaves you,
soft. The hard part,
the head, a tumbleweed of splinter and bone,
removed,
thinking it's made things easy for you.

That's its idea
of what love is, a thing without its head.

SNOWFLAKE

All thirty snowflakes stapled to the wall aren't real

Each one has been cut out of white paper by a small child

Some patterns had very simple lines, others more complex and full of holes

Everyone, even the children, know none of these are like the real thing

A real one begins somewhere out of their reach, formed by everything
outside itself

A real one doesn't last forever and ever like this

No one will talk about what will happen, what light will do to each one
outside

A VOLCANO

is

what happens

when you try

to take

the sun down

from where it is

You don't know it yet,

but here,

it won't come round

or be bound

to you

It will spill

itself out

into everything

and you,

you will wait for its light

to be put out,

wait to scrape out

the bits left

by its cooling over

A STARFISH

has

been cast out,

driven

from that higher place

Without light now

it sits

at the bottom of the ocean,

a kingdom

of its own arms,

looking back

at where it was

as where it was

looks back

at where it could be

LICHT

That's how they say light in Amsterdam

Like it's something you take into your mouth or begin to, something you can get close enough to lick

I thought light always had something to do with the eye, a thing you see when it's open

I never thought it could be something you could reach out for, pluck out of its place in the universe and its order

What if the sun tasted like orange sorbet? The kind served on a single glass spoon?

What if the sun isn't hot, if it has no heat, if it doesn't burn, if there are no bursts of fire or storms happening out there? Or anything, really, to fear up close?

If things aren't set, if in the order of things a law can come loose

You ain't nothin' but a big ol' clown
And I ain't gonna let you run this town

You come up ere thinkin' y'all big and round
Thinkin' you can run me inna ground

I ain't gonna let you run me outta this town
You best be turnin' that grin inna frown

You otta git goin', go, git on outta town
You just ain't ready for this here showdown

You just ain't nothin' but a big ol' clown
You best fix yerself up to leave this town

Woman on stage alone dressed in a checkered shirt and old torn-up pants. Patches of hair, glasses. The left lens is cracked, with a small hole.

I'm not much different, you know. Ma and Pa says so. I got a name. A good name. A real good name. (*Pause.*) See this checkad shirt? Pa gave it to me. And this stitch right here? Ma hemmed it when it busted. (*Excitedly.*) And I got titties too! (*Sticks chest out.*) See em? It's kinda hard to see em in this checkad shirt. But they're there, you know. They really are. Ma and Pa gave em to me. No, I ain't got no bra! Don't need one. (*Proudly.*) I let the wind take care of everythin. (*Pause.*) Besides, I ain't got time to doll myself up. It's not like anyone comes by here anyway. Just them birds. God dammit them birds! They fly away before I get a chance to say anythin! Some day one ain't gonna be so scared of me. (*Pushes glasses up. Smiles a bit.*) That'd be nice. Real nice. (*Pause.*) But I can't be botherin with such things 'cause I got a job to do. Keep em birds away and let things grow round here so we can keep the land. (*Pause.*) Me and this land we're the same. I'm made of it (*Pause.*) cept it's got pretty flowers growin on it sometimes and it's always green and when it ain't green it gets green. I'm its old stuff. All yellow and dried up and I don't get green. Ever. (*Long pause.*) No one comes out here much but Ma and Pa to check if I'm sittin up right. And sometimes Billy and…(*Casts eyes to ground.*) and his friends down the road. I been fixin up to take care of the land when they come on out here and start throwin rocks at me and settin fire. (*Touches patchy hair.*) It ain't right. I'm telling ya it just ain't right. See my left eye? (*Pushes up left lens.*) Ain't like it used to be. (*Long pause.*) But you know what?! God dammit! I got my other eye! And my titties too! (*Looks up at sky. Firmly.*) They can't take em.

1. When you think about the word light, what comes to mind first?

2. Do you work with real light (light from the sun) or only with electrical light?

3. What are you trying to do with light?

4. To do what you do, what are the tools you are in need of the most (i.e. screwdriver, wire, socket)?

5. What about the sun?

6. How about the eye?

7. How would you describe what you do? To someone who can't see? Would you describe it? In some ways, would you say that you can't see?

8. Do you think or work with the dark?

9. What can't you get light to do?

10. How do you talk about light (as something you see, could see, or something you need to create)?

11. Do words matter to you?

12. Would you say you describe or tell with light?

13. Why light?

JOULE

A joule is a unit of work and energy

A jewel is a gem, a thing you mine the earth for, a thing that occurs when laws and elements line up under the right conditions

To the ear, each alone, is the same

Only as written words do their differences come clear

The first letter: a hook, a drilled ground, a deep shaft

It's the letters that follow, their ordering set like layer and rock, element and time

The eye can discern this way, separate each to their difference don't have eyes

You look

at one;

look at where

the eyes

should be,

or could be;

and wonder,

if this here

is how

NOTES:

1. "Agnes Martin, Untitled #10" was written for *Poets Spell Art* at the Art Gallery of Ontario.

2. "Ljós": the two Icelandic words in this poem were given to me by a rawlings. Visit: http://arawlings.is/

3. "A Star" was printed and put inside a refurbished gum machine as part of the Toronto Poetry Vendors project. In 2011, it was available for two loonies and by chance.

4. "A thing I find impossible to lift": the title is taken from the last line of Elizabeth Bishop's "Five Flights Up."

CATHARINE NICHOLSON, "The Viable" (2008), pen and ink on watercolour paper.

Catharine wrote a short note about the picture: *A visual meditation on disease, and the chanciness of life. In 2008, a 54 year old Pedunculate oak tree on the edge of Cranborne Chase produced an extraordinarily rich crop of acorns, but almost all were infected by larval gall wasps. Such infections eventually destroy the acorn, consuming the internal soft tissue. In this picture there are forty-two acorns, forty-one of which have been fatally infected. Just one remains viable.*

JENNIFER ROWSOM

SOUVANKHAM THAMMAVONGSA was born in Nong Khai, Thailand in 1978. She won the 2004 ReLit prize for her first book, *Small Arguments*, as well as the Canadian Authors Association/Book Television award for best writer under thirty. Thammavongsa is also the author of *Found*, which was made into a short film and screened at film festivals worldwide, including the Toronto International Film Festival and Dok Leipzig.